TROPICAL FORESTS

Tom Jackson

www.heinemannraintree.com

Visit our website to find out more information about Heinemann-Raintree books.

To order:

☎ Phone 888-454-2279

✉ Visit www.heinemannraintree.com to browse our catalog and order online.

Published in 2011 by Heinemann-Raintree books, an imprint of Capstone Global Library, LLC, Chicago, Illinois

For The Brown Reference Group Ltd:
Editorial Director: Lindsey Lowe
Managing Editor: Tim Harris
Editor: Jolyon Goddard
Original consultant: Dr. Mark Hostetler,
Department of Wildlife Ecology and Conservation, University of Florida
Designers: Reg Cox, Joan Curtis
Picture researcher: Clare Newman
Production Director: Alastair Gourlay

Printed in the USA

ISBN: 978-1-432-94177-2; 978-1-432-94184-0 (set)
14 13 12 11 10
10 9 8 7 6 5 4 3 2 1

Library of Congress Cataloging-in-Publication Data

Jackson, Tom, 1972-
  Tropical forests / Tom Jackson.
    p. cm.—(Biomes atlases)
  Includes bibliographical references and index.
  ISBN 978-1-4329-4177-2 (hc)
  1. Rain forest ecology—Juvenile literature. 2. Rain forest ecology—Maps for children.
I. Title.
  QH541.5.R27J328 2011
  577.34—dc22   2010012915

About this Book

The introductory pages of this book describe the world's biomes and then the tropical forest biome. The five main chapters look at different aspects of tropical forests: climate, plants, animals, people, and the future. Between the chapters are detailed maps that focus on key forest areas. The map pages are shown in the contents in italics, *like this*. Exclamation-point icons on the map pages draw attention to regions where the biome or its wildlife is under threat. Throughout the book you'll also find boxed stories or fact files about tropical forests. The icons here show what the boxes are about. Words in **bold** throughout the book are explained in the glossary at the end of the book. After the glossary is a list of books and websites for further research and an index, allowing you to locate subjects anywhere in the book.

Climate

People

Plants

Future

Animals

Facts

Extinction

Under Threat

Contents

BIOMES OF THE WORLD

Biologists divide the living world into major zones named biomes. Each biome has its own distinctive climate, plants, and animals.

I f you were to walk all the way from the north of Canada to the Amazon **rain forest**, you'd notice the wilderness changing dramatically along the way (see route marked on map at right).

Northern Canada is a freezing and barren place without trees, where only tiny brownish-green plants can survive in the icy ground. But trudge south for long enough and you enter a magical world of conifer forests, where moose, caribou, and wolves live. After several weeks, the conifers disappear, and you reach the grass-covered prairies of the central United States. The farther south you go, the drier the land gets and the hotter the Sun feels, until you find yourself hiking through a cactus-filled desert. But once you reach southern Mexico, the cacti start to disappear, and strange tropical trees begin to take their place. Here, the muggy air is filled with the calls of exotic birds and the drone of **tropical** insects. Finally, in Colombia you cross the Andes mountain range—whose chilly peaks remind you a little of your starting point— and descend into the dense, swampy jungles of the Amazon rain forest.

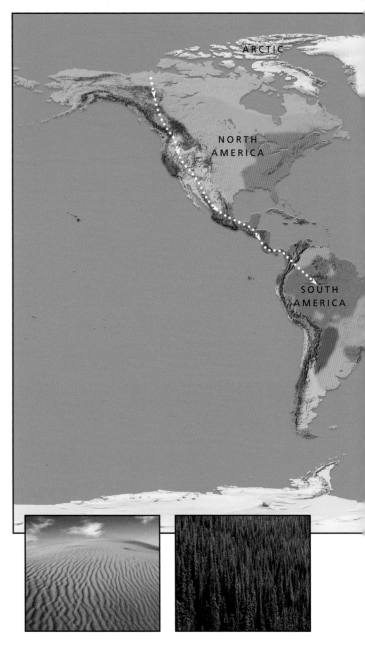

ARCTIC

NORTH AMERICA

SOUTH AMERICA

Desert is the driest biome. There are hot deserts and cold ones.

Taiga is made up of conifer trees that can survive freezing winters.

Scientists have a special name for the different regions—such as desert, tropical rain forest, and prairie—that you'd pass through on such a journey. They call them **biomes**. Everywhere on Earth can be classified as being in one biome or another, and the same biome often appears in lots of different

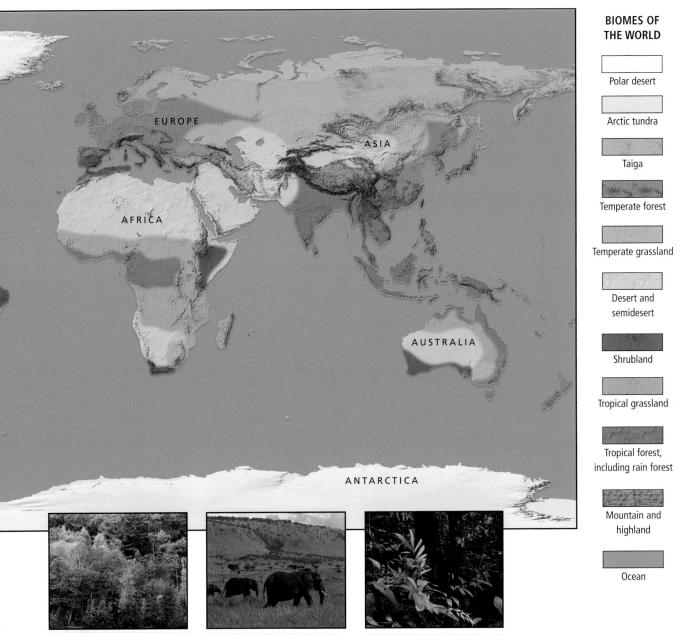

BIOMES OF THE WORLD

EUROPE

ASIA

AFRICA

AUSTRALIA

ANTARCTICA

Polar desert

Arctic tundra

Taiga

Temperate forest

Temperate grassland

Desert and semidesert

Shrubland

Tropical grassland

Tropical forest, including rain forest

Mountain and highland

Ocean

Temperate forest includes trees that lose their leaves in fall.

Tropical grassland, or savanna, is home to the biggest land animals.

Rain forest contains the richest mix of plants and animals on the planet.

places. For instance, there are areas of rain forest as far apart as Brazil, Africa, and Southeast Asia. Although the plants and animals that inhabit these forests are different, they live in similar ways. Likewise, the prairies of North America are part of the grassland biome, which also occurs in China, Australia, and Argentina. Wherever there are grasslands, there are grazing animals that feed on the grass, as well as large carnivores that hunt and kill the grazers.

The map on this page shows how the world's major biomes fit together to make up the biosphere—the zone of life on Earth.

TROPICAL FORESTS OF THE WORLD

Tropical forests are dark and humid, filled with tall trees and amazing animals. They grow in the tropics: the area of Earth between the Tropics of Cancer and Capricorn (*see map, right*).

Arctic circle

NORTH AMERICA

Tropic of Cancer

1

Equator

2

Tropic of Capricorn

☐ Tropical rain forest

■ Seasonal tropical forest

Antarctic circle

Unspoiled cloud forests still exist in Central America's mountains.

Deforestation threatens the vast rain forests of the Amazon basin.

The best-known type of **tropical forest** is tropical rain forest, which flourishes in places that are warm and rainy throughout the year. This kind of weather is perfect for plants, allowing them to keep their leaves and grow continuously, instead of dying or shedding their leaves in winter. Tropical rain forests are home to more plant **species** than any other biome—and they contain so many animal species that no one has even tried to count them. The biggest areas of tropical rain forest are in northern South America, central Africa, and Southeast Asia. There are also small patches of rain forest on rainy mountains, islands, and coasts throughout the tropics.

Most parts of the tropics have one or more wet seasons followed by a period of weeks or months when it hardly rains. Rain forests do not usually grow in places with a long dry season, but other types of tropical forest do. There are fewer tree species in these seasonal tropical forests, but the wildlife is still very rich. In some places the trees are **deciduous** —they shed their leaves for part of the year.

Not all rain forests grow in the tropics. Some forests in **temperate** (cool) countries are also called rain forests. There are temperate rain forests in very rainy parts

ASIA

AFRICA

3

4

5

6

SOUTH
AMERICA

AUSTRALIA

ANTARCTICA

| 3 | 4 | 5 | 6 |

Civil war and unrest in the Congo threaten much of its wildlife.

Seasonal tropical forest surrounds the ancient temples of Cambodia.

Southeast Asia's rain forests are home to the world's biggest flowers.

Waterfalls cascade from the densely forested slopes of New Guinea.

of Australia, New Zealand, South America, and North America. You can find out more about these forests in the *Taiga* and *Temperate Forests* books in this series.

Tropical forests have existed for more than 100 million years. Because they are so ancient, millions of species of plants and animals have evolved within them, and these species rely on each other in complex ways. As a result, tropical forests are fragile places. Since people started cutting down trees and introducing new species from elsewhere, the forests have begun to change, and many of their original inhabitants are dying out.

CENTRAL AMERICA

Most of Central America's forests have been felled to create farmland. There are still large stretches, however, in the humid lowlands of the east, and pockets of forest protected in the mountains.

Fact File

▲ Dotted through the jungles of Belize, Guatemala, and Mexico are ancient pyramids—temples built by the Mayan people more than 1,000 years ago.

▲ Central America is prone to hurricanes. One of the worst was Hurricane Mitch, which in 1998 killed more than 10,000 people.

▲ About 20 percent of Central America's tropical forests were cut down between 1990 and 2010.

1. Veracruz
The forest in this Mexican state is the most northerly moist tropical forest in the Americas. It is home to howler monkeys, kinkajous, agoutis, and pacas. Deforestation to make way for cattle ranches threatens the natural wildlife.

2. Petén
Guatemala's flat northern province is an unbroken sea of moist tropical forest. Flocks of endangered scarlet macaws squawk in the canopy, while ruined Mayan cities lie hidden below in the undergrowth. The region has suffered from severe deforestation in recent years.

3. Yucatán Peninsula
A flat area with patches of dry tropical forest and filled with cenotes (natural wells) and lagoons. Yucatán was central to the Mayan civilization. Again, deforestation threatens wildlife.

4. Cockscombe Basin Jaguar Reserve
Nestled in the Maya Mountains and administered by local people, this reserve was designed to be big enough to protect jaguars.

5. Monteverde Cloud Forest
This beautifully lush cloud forest on a volcano in Costa Rica is one of Central America's top attractions for ecotourists.

6. Reserva Biologica Absoluta de Cabo Blanco
One of several reserves in Costa Rica, it was set up to protect both coastal waters and tropical forest.

7. Mosquito Coast
This region is covered by untouched swampy forest.

8. Chirripo Grande
On a clear day, you can see both the east and west coasts of Central America from the summit of this mountain.

9. Darien Gap
The Pan-American Highway would join Alaska to southern Chile were it not for this 110-kilometer (70-mile) stretch of jungle. The Darien Gap includes national parks in both Panama and Colombia, and is a useful barrier that stops livestock diseases from passing between North and South America.

Some Central American countries are protecting their remaining forests in reserves, such as the Cordillera Volcanica Central Biosphere Reserve in Costa Rica.

Resplendent Quetzals

Quetzals are brilliantly colored birds that live in the forests of Central America. There are six species, and the aptly named resplendent quetzal is perhaps the most spectacular. The male (left) has vivid red and green plumage and a tail up to 1 meter (39 inches) long. Chiefs of the ancient Mayan civilization wore quetzal tail feathers as a sign of their authority. The resplendent quetzal lives only in the highlands of Central America. Little is known about the habits of this bird. It is now endangered due to loss of its forest habitat.

Atlantic Ocean

FLORIDA (U.S.)

Miami

Nassau

B A H A M A S

Gulf of Mexico

Tropic of Cancer

Havana

C U B A

Gulf of Mexico

Cancún

Yucatán Channel

CAYMAN ISLANDS

Chichén Itzá

Yucatán Peninsula

Sian Ka'an Biosphere Reserve

Caribbean

JAMAICA
Kingston

VERACRUZ

Mexico City
Puebla
Popocatépetl

Pantanos de Centla

TABASCO

M E X I C O

CHIAPAS

Sierra Madre

Tikal

BELIZE
Belmopan

Petén

Maya Mtns.

Cockscombe Basin Jaguar Reserve

Sea

Acapulco

GUATEMALA

Guatemala City

Tegucigalpa

HONDURAS

Rio Platano Biosphere Reserve

Mosquito Coast

San Salvador

EL SALVADOR

NICARAGUA

Managua

N

Pacific

NORTH AMERICA

SOUTH AMERICA

COSTA RICA

Monteverde Cloud Forest

San José

Cordillera Volcanica Central Biosphere Reserve

Chirripo Grande

Los Katios National Park

Colón

Panama City

Ocean

Reserva Biologica Absoluta de Cabo Blanco

PANAMA

Panama Canal

Darien National Park

COLOMBIA

0   300 miles
0   300   kilometers

TROPICAL FOREST CLIMATE

Tropical forests grow in parts of the world that are warm all year round and get lots of rain.

Tropical forests are warm because of their position on Earth's surface. They grow in the region around the **equator**—the imaginary line that divides Earth into northern and southern halves. In places close to the equator, the Sun shines down from high overhead in the middle of the sky for most of the day. However, in places far to the north and south of the equator, the Sun stays closer to the horizon (where the ground meets the sky), especially in the winter. You might notice this when you make a long journey from north to south. For example,

Rolling hills in the southeastern part of the Amazon rain forest trap banks of fog in the early mornings. The air here is humid for most of the year.

Small patches of tropical forest flourish on islands throughout the tropics, like this one in the Pacific. The warm sea makes the air humid (moist), creating frequent rain.

Driven by the Sun's heat, the humid air over the tropics rises high into the atmosphere. As the rising air cools, the moisture it carries condenses and forms clouds.

the southern state Florida is usually sunnier and warmer than the northern state Vermont —especially in winter.

To the north and south of the equator are two more imaginary lines: the **tropic of Cancer** to the north and the **tropic of Capricorn** to the south (*see* map, pages 6–7). These lines mark the boundaries of the region around the equator in which the Sun is high in the sky all year round. The area between the two lines is described as the tropics, and things that live there are tropical. In the tropics, the days are more or less the same length all year around, while away from these areas, days are long in summer and short in winter.

Invisible Water

The effect of the Sun being high in the sky is that more heat reaches tropical regions than cooler areas to the north and south. The Sun beating down warms the land, the air, and

Fact File

▲ Enough rain falls on the Amazon rain forest in a year to fill 2 billion Olympic-sized swimming pools.

▲ Tropical forest can soak up heavy rain, preventing floods. In Bangladesh, people have cut down so much forest for fuel or to make money that the country suffers devastating floods every few years.

▲ Scientists have found that during droughts smoke from forest fires stops rain clouds from forming, making the land even drier.

Right: Hurricane Katrina nears the coast of the Gulf of Mexico in 2005. More than 1,800 people lost their lives in the hurricane and the flooding that followed.

Main image: Seen from a space shuttle, vast storm clouds (cumulonimbus) form over southern Brazil. Thunderstorms are very common in the wet tropics.

the oceans. When water warms up, it begins to **evaporate**—it turns into an invisible gas, or vapor, that mixes with the air.

When air contains a lot of water vapor, we say it is humid. During a hot bath, the air in a bathroom gets very humid because the hot water produces lots of vapor. The air in tropical rain forests is as humid as that in a bathroom for much of the day. The warmth and humidity can be uncomfortable, making people feel sweaty, hot, and tired.

Warm air rises. At the equator, warm air is rising nearly all the time, carrying water vapor high into the sky. As the humid air gets higher, it cools down, which makes the vapor turn back into liquid water. The water forms towering rain clouds and falls to the ground as heavy rain. Often the rain comes in violent storms, followed by periods of calm, sweaty conditions.

Tropical Seasons

On average, Earth's equator gets more strong sunlight than anywhere else, so it is the warmest and most humid part of the planet—and therefore the rainiest. A belt of rainy weather roughly encircles the equator, as the maps on this page show.

This rain belt changes position slightly during the year. It moves because Earth is tilted, which causes the amount of sunlight falling on the tropics to vary during the year. In July the North Pole tilts toward the Sun, so the tropic of Cancer gets stronger sunlight than the equator. As a result, the belt of rainy weather moves north a bit. In January the opposite happens: The

South Pole tilts toward the Sun, and the tropic of Capricorn gets more sunlight than the equator. So the rain belt moves south.

Places very near the equator stay under the rain belt for most of the year, though there might be a "dry" season when it rains less

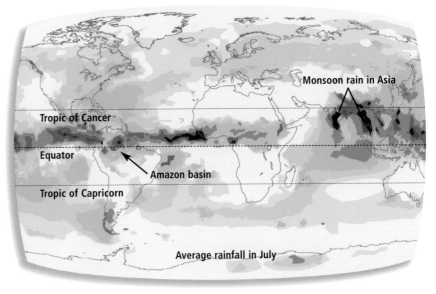

A belt of rainy weather (blue) surrounds the equator. It moves north in summer (above) and south in winter (below), creating wet and dry seasons.

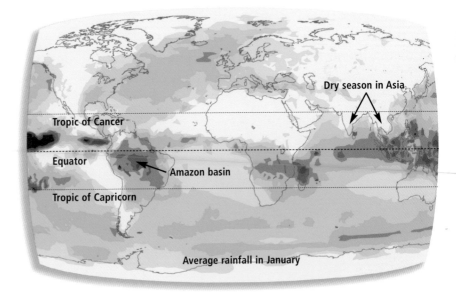

often. These places, such as the Amazon basin, are where rain forests flourish. As much as 2,500 millimeters (100 inches) of rain can fall on a rain forest in an average year—that's five times as much rain as San Francisco gets.

Wildfires

In many parts of the tropics, the rainy season is unreliable. Every few years, the rains fail to fall in large enough quantities, causing a drought. As the forest dries out, the risk of a raging wildfire gets greater and greater. We all know how forest fires can sweep through dry areas of the United States and burn for weeks on end. In the tropics, they are even worse. Worldwide, as much as 130,000 square kilometers (50,000 square miles) of tropical forest may be lost to fires in a dry year. In 2005, a severe drought in the Amazon Basin resulted in many rivers drying up and thousands of forest fires.

In contrast, other parts of the tropics move in and out of the rain belt. These places have a significant dry season each year, which has a huge influence on the wildlife.

Places with a very long dry season don't get enough rain for forests. Instead, grass takes over, forming **savanna** (tropical grassland with scattered trees). Places with a shorter dry season have seasonal tropical forests, which are different from rain forests. The trees are shorter, less tightly packed, and many are deciduous—they shed their leaves and stop growing for part of the year.

Monsoons

The biggest area of seasonal tropical forest is in southern Asia. The forest there is called **monsoon** forest because of an unusually intense rainy season termed the monsoon.

The monsoon is caused by a wind that blows in one direction during summer and the opposite way in winter. The summer wind blows north from the Indian Ocean, bringing lots of humidity and rain. This wet season lasts from May to the end of September. The winter wind blows south off Asia and is much drier.

The wind itself is caused by a difference in the way Earth's land and sea warm up during the year. Land warms up quickly under the summer sunshine, but it cools down just as quickly in winter. In contrast, the oceans warm up and cool down slowly.

During summer the vast landmass of Asia warms up enormously because of its size. As a result, air starts rising over it. Moister air from the ocean—the monsoon wind—rushes inland to take the place of the rising air. As it crosses the land, it dumps its moisture as heavy rain. In India it can pour down every day for weeks during the monsoon.

The temple of Angkor Wat in Cambodia is surrounded by seasonal tropical forest. The trees are not as tall or densely packed as in a rain forest.

Climographs

Each place in the world has its own pattern of weather. The typical pattern of weather that happens in one place during a year is called climate. We can sum up a place's climate on a climograph, such as the one shown here for St. Louis. The letters along the bottom are the months of the year. The numbers on the left and the small bars show rainfall, and the numbers on the right and the curvy line show temperature. You can see at a glance that St. Louis is hottest in July, but December is the driest month.

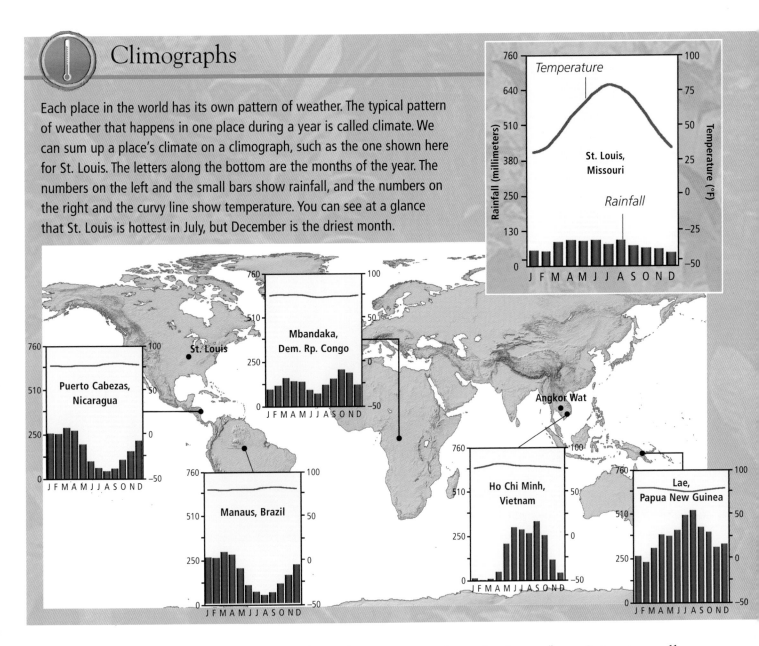

In winter the landmass of Asia cools, and the air above it starts sinking. The sinking air spreads outward, causing a dry wind to blow south from Asia toward the Indian Ocean. During the dry season, there may be no rain at all for months.

Winds that change direction between seasons in other parts of the world are also called monsoons. The rains that fall on Arizona and New Mexico in summer are carried by a monsoon wind, for example.

Microclimates

Inside a tropical forest, temperature and humidity vary from place to place. The treetops, for instance, are sunnier and warmer than the forest floor. Scientists call the different conditions found in various parts of the forest "microclimates."

Microclimates include more than just temperature and humidity. Light levels, wind speeds, and the amounts of the gases **oxygen** and **carbon dioxide** also vary from place to place in the forest. The large range of microhabitats in tropical forests is one of the reasons there are so many species.

Tropical forests do not have summers and winters, but the change in conditions from day to night can be almost as great as the change between these two seasons in many other parts of the world. During the day, it is warm and bright. This is when the plants grow fastest,

15

just as they would in summer. By contrast, the nights are cooler and darker, and most plants do not grow very much, as if it were winter. The difference between daytime and nighttime temperatures can be larger than the difference between the average temperatures in January and July in many cooler regions of the world.

Cloud Forests

The weather on mountains is always different from weather in the lowlands. In the tropics, the lowlands are often hot and humid, with little breeze. Mountains are usually cooler and windier, making the air feel fresher. On a single mountain, the weather can vary a great deal—one side might be wet and rainy, while the other is as dry as a desert.

Some tropical mountains always seem to be shrouded in mist, even when the weather

Right: Floods are a frequent problem in Chittagong, Bangladesh, during the monsoon season. Deforestation in recent years has made the problem worse.

Under the Waterfall

In the heart of southern Africa, the mighty Zambezi River plunges into a gigantic chasm in the ground, forming one of the biggest and most spectacular waterfalls on Earth: Victoria Falls. This breathtaking waterfall is twice as wide and twice as deep as Niagara Falls in North America. Although the land around the waterfall is savanna, patches of rain forest grow on the cliffs around the falls. The forest is watered not by rain but by the constant spray thrown up as the river thunders over the edge.

Many of the animals and plants in this unique microclimate are the same as those found in central Africa's rain forests hundreds of miles to the north. There are palms, ebony trees, and strangler figs, for example, as well as the magnificent trumpeter hornbill, a fruit-eating bird that also lives in the Congo forests.

below is dry and clear. Strange and enchanting forests grow in such places, their plants thriving on the moisture-laden air. They are called **cloud forests**.

Cloud forests are as lush and green as lowland rain forests, but the plants are different. The trees are shorter and often crooked. Smaller plants called **epiphytes**, which hang from the trees' branches and cling to their trunks, are much more conspicuous in cloud forests than in lowland rain forests. The epiphytes grow so thickly that the whole forest appears to be dripping with plant life. One of the world's biggest areas of cloud forest is on the Virunga and Ruwenzori mountains of central Africa—home to the endangered mountain gorilla.

At 1,430 meters (4,700 feet) above sea level, Monteverde cloud forest in Costa Rica is often wrapped in clouds. This reserve is home to more than 400 orchid species.

AMAZON RAIN FOREST

The Amazon rain forest is as large as all of the United States from the Rockies to the Atlantic Ocean. It occupies a vast, flat river basin filled with branches of the mighty Amazon River.

The mighty rivers of the Amazon basin flood an area of forest the size of Louisiana every rainy season. Birds, monkeys, and insects continue life in the canopy, while river dolphins, fish, and caimans swim among the tree roots.

Fact File

▲ With few roads, much of the endless Amazon rain forest is inaccessible and unexplored.

▲ Early explorers described it as an area where water and land had swapped places—the wide, smooth rivers are easy to move along, while the dense forest is mostly impassable.

▲ At the current rate of deforestation, 40 percent of the Amazon rain forest will have been cut down and cleared by 2030.

Slow but Sure

Six species of sloths live in Central and South American rain forests. They move so slowly that algae (plantlike organisms) grow in their fur, giving the sloths a greenish tinge. Sloths rarely venture to the ground, even giving birth up trees. Their diet of leaves and twigs contains very few nutrients, so they conserve energy by moving very slowly; they spend most of their time hanging motionless while digesting their food. If deforestation continues at its present rate, sloths will soon become threatened.

1. Andes
Many of the region's rivers begin in the Andes mountains.

2. Rio Abiseo National Park, Peru
The last refuge of the yellow-tailed woolly monkey and the tiny mouse opossum.

3. Flooded Forest
On the flat bottom of the Amazon basin, the rivers flood huge areas of nearby forest to a depth of up to 10 meters (30 feet). Logging threatens this unique habitat.

4. Madidi National Park
This park contains more than 900 species of birds.

5. Angel Falls
The world's highest waterfall tumbles off the sheer side of a table mountain and plummets into the jungle below. Mining threatens to disrupt wildlife in the region around the falls.

6. Manaus
Located in the heart of the rain forest, Manaus was originally the center of Brazil's rubber industry. The city's expanding population is clearing forest to settle.

7. Amazon River
Earth's largest river flows through the heart of the forest. Plans to dam some of the river's tributaries would result in vast areas of forest becoming flooded.

8. Guiana Highlands
The forests on these low mountains remain pristine, safe from loggers because the area is so difficult to get to.

9. Central Suriname Nature Reserve
An undeveloped hilly area where animals such as jaguars, giant armadillos, tapirs, and sloths are protected, as well as 400 species of birds and 8 species of monkeys.

10. Belém
A large port at the mouth of the Amazon, where the river meets the ocean, 6,400 kilometers (4,000 miles) from the source.

PLANTS OF THE FOREST

The tropical climate is ideal for plants, but life is still tough. Forest plants are crowded together and battle with each other to survive.

The number of plants in a tropical rain forest is staggering. Plants don't just grow from the soil—they also grow on the trees, and a few tiny ones even grow on the plants that are growing on the trees. Most plants grow well when they have plenty of sunlight, lots of water, and a warm climate. Tropical rain forests are like this all year round—that's why so many plants grow in them.

Epiphytes are plants that grow on other plants. They get all their moisture from the air or rain.

Getting Light

Trees are the kings of the forest. Other plants must live in their shadow. Many rain-forest trees are among the tallest plants in the world—the klinki pine of New Guinea grows to 92 meters (302 feet) —almost as tall as the Statue of Liberty.

Trees win the battle for light by growing above the other plants. Unlike the trees you might see in your park, rain-forest

Right: Sunlight breaks through the canopy of a tropical rain forest in northern Australia. Rain-forest plants grow so densely that little light reaches the forest floor.

trees typically have tall trunks with few low branches. At the top, a mass of branches spreads out into a broad crown. Together, all the crowns form a thick layer of leaves called the canopy, which soaks up the Sun's rays. A few giant trees, called emergents, are taller than the canopy and poke out of the top. Like many rain-forest trees, emergents often have buttress roots—huge, spreading roots that grow out from the base of the trunk and support the tree's weight (*see* page 24).

Underneath the canopy it is much darker, but many plants manage to survive in this shady world. Some, like ferns, simply make do with the weak, greenish light that filters through the canopy. Others are cheats—they hitch a ride on other plants.

Hitching a Ride

Plants that grow on other plants are called epiphytes. They sprout and take root in nooks and crannies on the trunks and branches of trees, where they are much closer to the light than are plants of the forest floor.

Some epiphytes sprout in the canopy, but others climb to get there. The roots of such epiphytes stick to bark, and the plant grows steadily toward the light. As the ends of the roots die away, the whole plant creeps gradually up the tree, like a very slow snail.

Other climbers, such as lianas, start from the ground but lean on a tree for support. With no need to produce a trunk of their own, their wiry stems quickly shoot up to the canopy. Once there, they grow a crown that can be as big as that of the supporting tree, throwing it into shade and weakening it.

Lianas can grow hundreds of yards long in tropical rain forests. As they tangle their way through the canopy, they tie lots of trees

Number of plant species per 100 kilometer (62 mile) square

- less than 100
- 100–200
- 200–500
- 500–1,000
- 1,000–1,500
- 1,500–2,000
- 2,000–3,000
- 3,000–4,000
- 4,000–5,000
- more than 5,000

NORTH AMERICA

SOUTH AMERICA

Andes

EUROPE

AFRICA

Sahara

ASIA

Himalayas

New Guinea

AUSTRALIA

Forest Hot Spots

The colors on this map show how many plant species there are in different parts of the world. Red and pink places have the most plant species, while yellow areas have the fewest.

You can see at a glance that tropical forests contain some of the richest areas of plant life on Earth, with far more species than deserts or the forests of Europe or North America. The areas with the greatest diversity of plants are where tropical forests meet mountains, such as the Andes in South America, the Himalayas in Asia, or the mountains of New Guinea.

Mountains are very diverse habitats, with complex weather and different plants and animals living at varying heights. That's why they support such a variety of species.

together. They are especially common in open areas, such as riverbanks. People sometimes use lianas as a source of water—they chop them open with a machete and drink the clear water that dribbles out.

Stranglehold

Strangler figs are climbing plants that kill the trees they grow on. They start life as epiphytes growing from seeds left high in the branches by an animal. As a strangler's leaves climb up toward the light, its roots grow down to the ground and wrap around the tree's trunk. As the strangler gets bigger, more roots twist around the trunk, surrounding it with a lattice of roots that appears to be strangling the tree within. Meanwhile, the strangler's crown grows so big that it casts a shadow over the tree, killing it. The tree's trunk eventually rots away, but the strangler stays standing. Its network of roots now form a hollow trunk that is strong enough to hold up the mature crown.

A strangler fig chokes its victim in a Belize rain forest. The tree inside will die and rot away, leaving a hollow.

Lianas provide a handy means of getting around the rain forests of Sumatra. Despite their agility, orangutans suffer many falls from the trees.

Water, Water Everywhere

For plants in many biomes, getting water is often a challenge. But for the trees in a rain forest, the problem is sometimes the opposite—they have to cope with frequent downpours. If too much water collects on the leaves, it weighs down the branches or causes mold to grow. So, many rain-forest trees have smooth leaves that repel water and pointed leaf tips that help water dribble off.

Plants get water through their roots. Though rain-forest trees are huge, their roots are mostly less than 60 centimeters (2 feet) deep—much shallower than the roots of temperate-forest trees. Because of the shallow roots, rain-forest trees are prone to fall over in storms, so some have stiltlike roots that prop them up. The buttress roots of emergents also help them withstand storms. Although shallow, the roots of rain-forest trees often spread very widely from the base of the tree.

Up in the Air

Epiphytes don't start life on the ground, so they have to get their water elsewhere. Many have roots that collect rain dribbling down the tree, and many can absorb water from the humid air. Most epiphytes have thick, leathery leaves or swollen stems that store water. Some, called tank bromeliads, collect water in a tiny pond. Tank bromeliads have a rosette of spiky leaves like the cluster of leaves on a pineapple. The leaf bases overlap,

This tropical mistletoe is a parasite. It grows on trees and has roots that burrow into its host to steal water and nutrients.

forming a bowl that traps rainwater. Some frogs lay their eggs in these bromeliad ponds, and the tadpoles develop inside them.

Some epiphytes are **parasites**—they steal food and water from another plant. Parasitic epiphytes drive their roots into the host tree to tap into its veins. Some parasites have their own leaves for making food, as well.

Getting Nutrients

Plants don't just need water and light to survive—they also need chemicals called nutrients, which they get from rotting animal and plant remains in the soil. The soil in a tropical forest forms from animal droppings, dead leaves, fragments of wood, and dead animals. Fungi, bacteria, and insects break this mixture down, turning it into a damp compost and releasing the nutrients. Because tropical forests are often warm and wet, the rotting matter breaks down very quickly, and the trees absorb the nutrients almost as soon as they are released. As a result, the soil in a tropical forest is surprisingly shallow and low in nutrients—temperate forests have much thicker, richer soil. If rotting matter was not constantly replacing nutrients, the soil would soon run out of them and nothing would grow.

Epiphytes somehow have to get nutrients from high in the trees. Some collect falling bits of debris, which slowly build up into a thin layer of soil. Those that steal water from their host tree get a free supply of nutrients dissolved in the water.

Buttress roots give rain-forest trees extra support. Because rain forests have shallow soil, most trees have wide, spreading roots rather than deep ones.

Saving the Planet

The government of Peru, worried by the rate of destruction of its Amazonian rain forest, adopted a strategy to halt the decline. Its policy meant allocating specific regions for legal logging, giving complete protection to other tracts of forest, and establishing territories for indigenous peoples. The plan seems to have worked, and large-scale rain forest damage was checked after 1999. Constant monitoring is necessary to ensure continued success.

Flower Power

Flowers are not just for decoration—they enable plants to reproduce sexually. Flowers produce male cells and female cells. When a male cell from one flower joins with a female cell from another flower, the united cells grow into an embryo (the beginnings of a new plant), and a **seed** forms around this.

This might sound straightforward, but there's a snag: Unlike animals, plants can't move around to find a mate. They have other ways of making sure that male and female cells from different plants join together. The most common solution is to make **pollen**, a dustlike substance that carries the male cells from one flower to another. When pollen lands on the female part of a flower, it sprouts and grows down into the flower to deliver the male cell. This process is termed **pollination**.

Finding a Partner

Pollination is tricky in tropical forests because there are so many different species. A plant can reproduce only with other members of its species, but the nearest mate may be miles away. Among many of the tall tree species, the wind carries pollen. The trees' flowers release vast amounts of tiny pollen grains into the air. Most blow away and get lost, but a few grains settle on exactly the right flowers somewhere else in the forest.

Beneath the canopy, the air is too still for wind pollination. Instead, flying animals carry the pollen between flowers. In return for this service, the animals receive nectar, a sugary liquid produced by flowers. A few animals also eat some of the pollen.

Red-eyed tree frogs clamber over a Heliconia *plant in Belize.* Heliconia *flowers are usually pollinated by hummingbirds.*

Getting Noticed

Flying insects, such as bees, beetles, butterflies, and moths, are the most common animal pollinators. Many flowers have a specific shape that suits a certain type of pollinator. For example, flowers that beetles pollinate are broad and dish-shaped, allowing these large insects to scramble about as they gather nectar. As they do so, pollen sticks to them, ready to rub off on the next flower.

Bee flowers open during the day, when bees are busiest. Such flowers are often brightly colored, with lines that direct the bee toward the pollen. Butterfly flowers are usually funnel-shaped. To reach the nectar at the base of the funnel, a butterfly uses a very long mouthpart that works like a straw. When the butterfly isn't feeding, the mouthpart coils up under its head. Moths feed like butterflies, but at night. Their flowers are often white and scented so they are easy to find in the dark.

Some flowers are pollinated by birds and bats. Bird flowers are usually red and are tough because birds are much larger than

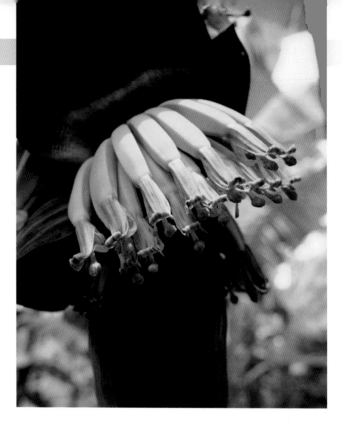

Banana flowers are pollinated by bats. Wild banana plants produce fruit and seeds after pollination. Cultivated banana plants (right) produce seedless fruit—the bananas we buy from supermarkets.

insects. Hummingbirds hover beside their flowers, flapping their wings up to 70 times a second to keep perfectly still while they probe for nectar with their bill. Bats feed at night, so their flowers are often pale and have a musty scent. Most bat flowers look a little like brushes—when a bat pays a visit, the brush gives its chest a dusting of pollen.

Many birds and bats are too big to fly into the middle of a plant, so their flowers are usually positioned on the outside of the plant. Banana flowers are like this and are usually pollinated by bats.

Spreading Out

Once a plant has produced its seeds, it can't just drop them onto the ground. If they sprouted there, the young plants would soon end up crowded together, competing with each other and their parent for light, nutrients, and water. Most plants, therefore, have ways of dispersing their seeds. Although many go to waste in the crowded forest, a few stand a good chance of finding just the right place to start life.

Many of the tallest trees produce seeds with wings, which make the seeds spin around in the air, slowing their fall. When such seeds are released from the high treetops, they can travel a long way on the breeze. However, most tropical forest plants have a different strategy to spread their seeds: They bribe animals to carry the seeds away.

The usual way of doing this is by enclosing the seed in an edible fruit. Animals eat the fruit, swallow the seeds, and move off into the forest. When the seeds eventually pass out of the animal's body, they are far from the parent plant. They land on the ground in a heap of droppings—a perfect fertilizer for the young plants.

A snowcap hummingbird hovers over a wild poinsettia flower to sip nectar. This tiny bird from Central America is 6 centimeters (2.5 inches) long—people often mistake it for an insect.

Biggest Flower in the World

The world's largest flower belongs to a peculiar plant called *Rafflesia arnoldii*, which grows only in the rain forests of Sumatra. In some ways *Rafflesia* is more like a fungus than a plant. It has no true roots, stems, or leaves, and it cannot make its own food. Instead, it lives as a parasite, sending fine, theadlike growths into vines to steal water and nutrients. The only part of *Rafflesia arnoldii* that you can see is its gigantic red and white flower, which grows to 1 meter (39 inches) wide on the forest floor. Even the flower is weird. It smells of rotting flesh, attracting flies that normally lay eggs on dead animals. Tricked by the foul stench, the flies unwittingly pollinate the flower.

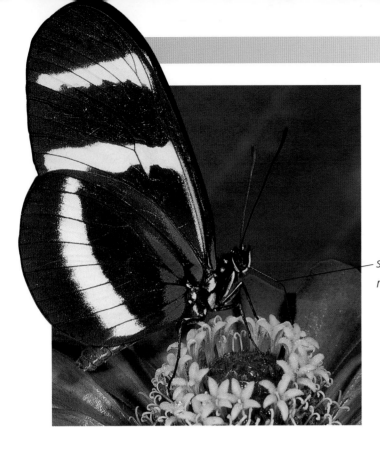

sucking mouthpart

Above: With its slender mouthpart unrolled, a postman butterfly sucks nectar from a flower in Costa Rica.

In temperate climates, plants that produce fruit or nuts all tend to do so at the end of summer. In a tropical rain forest, different types of fruit come into season at different times of the year. Because fruit and nuts are usually available somewhere in the forest, many animals specialize in eating little else. They include fruit bats, many monkeys, and birds such as parrots, toucans, and hornbills. Such animals usually move around a lot as they search for the few trees with ripe fruit.

Stinky Fruit

Durians are large, spiky fruits that look like giant horse chestnuts. Although the flesh of this fruit is sweet, the fruit has a very strong, rotten odor. Some people don't mind the smell and eat the fruit, but many more can't bear it. The stinky fruit is even banned on the subway in Singapore, Southeast Asia. In the forest, however, the powerful smell attracts tigers, orangutans, and many other animals, all of which eagerly devour the custardlike flesh.

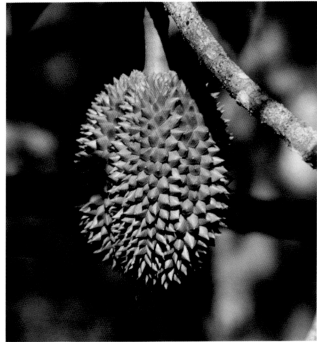

Above: Durians smell revolting to us, but many animals, from orangutans to tigers, find them delicious.

Awaiting the Gap

Once a seed has been carried across the forest, dropped in a perfect patch of soil, and sprouted into a sapling (baby tree), it faces a new challenge: lack of light. The floor of a tropical forest is usually dark and gloomy, so how can a sapling get the light it needs to grow all the way to the canopy?

For many trees, the answer is to wait. After reaching a couple of meters tall, the saplings stop growing. They can wait for years like this, absorbing just enough energy from the dim light to keep themselves alive. Their big chance comes when a large tree falls down, creating a gap in the canopy that lets sunlight flood onto the forest floor.

Once a gap opens, the saplings race upward in a fierce contest to fill the empty space. Eventually, one wins, and the gap disappears. Some small plants grow only in gaps. They flower and set seed quickly, before the forest closes in again, and their seeds lie ready in the soil for the next gap to form.

Banyan Trees

Producing seeds enables trees to spread to new places, but some tropical trees can spread where they stand—by growing sideways. The banyan tree, a native of tropical Asia, produces aerial roots that grow down from its branches. When they reach the ground, they become new trunks. A single banyan tree can spread indefinitely this way, turning into a thicket or even a small forest. One banyan tree in Hawaii covers nearly 0.4 hectares (1 acre).

CONGO RAIN FOREST

The Congo rain forest lies in a vast river basin straddling the equator in central Africa. The heart of the forest is a largely unspoiled wilderness, where only rivers and occasional clearings break the canopy.

The swampy clearings, or bais, *of the Congo region are like magnets to wildlife. Animals such as forest elephants and lowland gorillas visit them to eat roots, grass, and minerals. The* bais *allow scientists to study the animals before they melt back into the forest.*

Congo Facts

▲ Most of Africa's rain forest is in or around the Congo basin, but there is also rain forest in parts of west Africa, including Liberia and Ivory Coast.

▲ The central part of the Congo rain forest is so swampy and difficult to reach that it remains almost untouched by loggers and farmers.

▲ One of the main threats to the forest wildlife is poaching. Poachers hunt elephants for ivory. They also kill animals for their meat.

▲ Deforestation by farmers and loggers is a growing problem in outer parts of the Congo basin.

▲ The Bronx Zoo in New York houses a 2.6-hectare (6.5-acre) reconstruction of Congo rain forest, complete with more than 20 gorillas, 11 waterfalls, and 15,000 plants of nearly 400 species.

1. Taï National Park
One of the last major remnants of primary tropical rain forest in west Africa. Its chimps use rocks to crack open nuts.

2. Dja Faunal Reserve
One of the best-protected rain forests in Africa. The Dja River surrounds it, forming a natural barrier.

3. Congo River
Africa's second-longest river after the Nile. Plans for dams will result in the flooding of vast areas of forest.

4. Salonga National Park
One of the largest national parks on Earth, home to forest elephants and bonobos. War in the region threatens wildlife.

5. Congo Basin
Much of this vast area of lowland rain forest, swamps, and winding rivers floods in the rainy season. Poaching puts many of its animals at risk.

6. Virunga National Park
One of the last refuges of mountain gorillas, the largest primates in the world. War in neighboring Rwanda (1990–1993) drove refugees into Virunga, resulting in deforestation and poaching. Ongoing hostilities in the region still threaten wildlife.

7. Ituri Forest
Dramatic scenery and tumbling waterfalls make this hilly corner of the Congo very beautiful. The Mbuti people live in this forest.

8. Okapi Wildlife Reserve
Home to 5,000 of the world's 20,000 remaining wild okapis—short-necked relatives of giraffes with striped legs. In 2005, fighting in the region put the okapis at risk.

9. Gombe Stream National Park
A woodland reserve famous for its chimpanzees. Scientists have been studying their complex social behavior for decades.

10. Lake Victoria
Africa's largest lake is the main source of the White Nile, which flows north to the Nile River. The region around Lake Victoria is one of the most densely populated parts of Africa.

Bonobos

One of the Congo rain forest's most interesting animals is the bonobo, or pygmy chimpanzee, which lives only to the south of the Congo River. Despite its name, it is no smaller than its cousin the common chimpanzee.

Scientists think bonobos (right) are descended from a group of chimpanzees that crossed the Congo River from north to south about 1.5 million years ago. Isolated by the river and its swamps, the group evolved separately. Common chimpanzees live in aggressive, male-dominated societies. In contrast, bonobos live in more peaceful, female-dominated societies. This species is endangered. There are conservation efforts to protect bonobos, although ongoing unrest in the Congo region has led to a serious decline in the numbers of this ape.

ANIMALS OF THE FOREST

Tropical forests teem with an amazing number of weird and wonderful animals, from flying frogs and birds of paradise to giant millipedes and midget hippos. They are also home to some of the most colorful animals on Earth.

Nobody knows how many animal species live on Earth, but one thing's certain: A lot of them live in tropical forests. One scientist collected beetles from just 19 trees in the rain forest of Panama. He counted nearly 1,000 species, so the total number of tropical beetles worldwide could be millions. Beetles probably outnumber most other animal species, but tropical forests are still home to countless other insects and spiders, not to mention snakes, monkeys, bats, birds, frogs, cats, anteaters, and all kinds of other animals.

Blue-and-yellow macaws are a common sight in the Amazon rain forest. These birds form very strong bonds with each other and are often seen in pairs.

Grasping toes and flexible ankle joints allow kinkajous to hang by their feet while searching for food. They live in Central and South America.

Animal Niches

You might wonder how so many species could survive in such a crowded place—surely they'd end up eating each other's food and getting in each other's way? They avoid such problems because each animal species has its own particular way of life, or **niche**. It eats certain foods, lives in a particular part of the forest, and uses unique skills to survive.

A niche is not just the animal's home in the forest, such as the canopy or a rotting log. It is a combination of habitat, behavior, and time. For example, an animal that feeds at night has a different niche from one that feeds during the day. Likewise, two species of bats might fly around the same sorts of plants in search of insects to eat, but one might prefer large moths while the other eats flies. Each bat, therefore, has its own niche.

Toucans (above) live in South America, while hornbills (right) live in Africa. They have evolved into species that fill similar niches in forests thousands of miles apart.

Forest Midgets

Many of the mammals that live in tropical forests are smaller than their relatives from more open country. These small animals are often called pygmies. Africa's Congo rain forest is home to pygmy hippos and maybe also pygmy elephants. Pygmy elephants are believed to be a population of small forest elephants and half the size of savanna elephants. Pygmy hippos are one-tenth the weight of other hippos (but still three times heavier than a person). Rhinoceroses in Asian forests are also smaller than their grassland relatives in Africa, and deer in some rain forests are as small as rabbits.

One reason forest mammals are small is that it helps them move through undergrowth. Another is that there is more high-energy food, such as fruit, in forests. Small mammals need a constant supply of energy, but larger mammals digest and use their food more slowly. Savanna elephants grow to a huge size while eating large quantities of poor-quality food.

Tropical forests are complex places, with millions of different niches. This is why so many animal species can coexist in them.

Similar but Different

Tropical forests in different parts of the world have very different sets of animals, but they often have similar niches. As a result, unrelated animals have become similar through evolution. Scientists call this process convergent evolution.

One example is the similarity of South America's toucans to the hornbills thousands of kilometers away in Africa and Asia. Both types of birds have spectacularly long bills, which they use to break open nuts and fruits.

Another pair of animals that look and behave the same way but live on the opposite sides of the world are the pudu and mouse deer. Pudus live in the forests of South America, where they feed on fruit. They are only 30 centimeters (1 foot) long—about the same size as rabbits. They share the title of world's smallest deer with mouse deer, which live in the forests of Malaysia, in Southeast Asia. They, too, are no bigger than rabbits and feed

Southeast Asia's slow lorises come out at night to look for insects and fruit, using their large eyes to see in the gloom. To avoid being spotted by predators, they do everything in slow motion.

on fruit. These deer species have evolved in similar ways because they occupy similar niches in the rain forest.

Sometimes a niche is filled by a completely different type of animal. For example, there are no monkeys or lemurs in the tropical forests of Australia, so the fruit-eating niche is filled mainly by birds, especially parrots and pigeons.

Monkey Business

Monkeys are perhaps the most familiar of forest animals. These agile creatures live all over the forest from the highest branches in the treetops to the forest floor and along the edges of rivers. Monkeys belong to a larger group of animals called **primates**, nearly all of which live in tropical forests. Besides

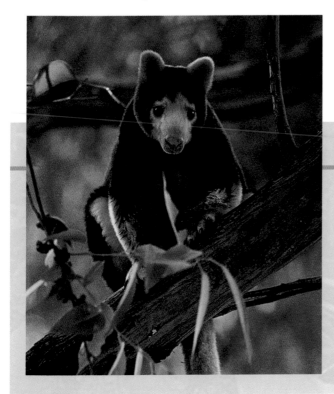

monkeys, the primate group includes apes, lemurs, and smaller animals called bushbabies, tarsiers, and lorises. Apes are generally bigger than monkeys, with longer arms and no tails. Gorillas, chimpanzees, orangutans, gibbons, and humans are all apes. Lemurs are easy to tell apart from monkeys because they have catlike faces with long snouts. They live only on the island of Madagascar, where there are no monkeys. Bushbabies, lorises, and tarsiers are small, **nocturnal** (night-active) primates with huge eyes for seeing in the dark. While monkeys,

Tree Kangaroo

Although there are no monkeys in the forests of Australia and New Guinea, other mammals have taken to the trees. One of the most surprising is the tree kangaroo, a relative of the more familiar kangaroos that hop around on the ground. The tree kangaroo has more muscular arms and wider feet than its ground-dwelling cousins. It uses the claws on its hands to grip branches, and it can "walk" by moving its back legs alternately —something other kangaroos cannot do on land. It can also hop along the ground when it needs to.

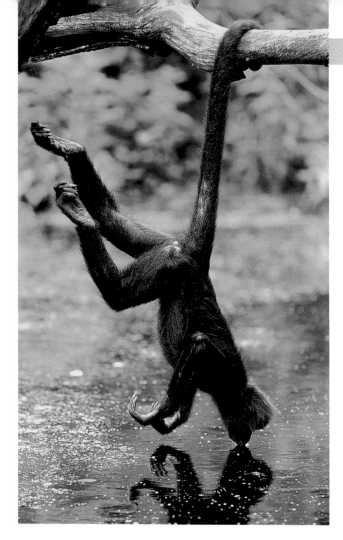

In Central and South America, many of the monkeys have a tail that is prehensile—it can wrap around things and be used as a fifth limb. Spider monkeys (left) have tails strong enough to support their whole body weight. Their prehensile tails help them move, but spider monkeys can also swing from branch to branch like gibbons, using their thumbless hands as hooks.

High-ranking male mandrills have very bright blue and red marks on their face as a display of status. These marks grow darker when a male is spoiling for a fight.

The world's smallest monkey—the pygmy marmoset—weighs a mere 90 grams (3 ounces) and could sit on your hand. This diminutive primate lives in the northern parts of the Amazon rain forest. While large monkeys swing through the trees, pygmy marmosets are small enough to perch on blades of grass.

apes, and lemurs tend to live in social groups, most of the nocturnal primates live on their own or with their offspring.

Large and Small

The world's largest monkey is the mandrill, which lives on the floor of Africa's Congo rain forest. A fully grown male mandrill weighs about as much as an eight-year-old child, while females are half the weight of males. Male monkeys are often larger than females because they have to fight with each other to win mates.

Like many primates, mandrills live in social groups with a ranking system. The top-ranking male usually gets more mating opportunities than his rivals in the group.

Only adult males sport the bright markings for which mandrills are famous. Blue and crimson patches of skin on the buttocks complement those on the face.

Above: Lemurs spends most of their time in the trees. Sifakas are lemurs that make spectacular leaps from tree to tree, but their jumping style of movement seems clumsy on the ground. This mother carries her baby.

Below: Pygmy marmosets are the world's smallest monkeys. They are nervous animals and move in a quick, jerky manner. Unlike most monkeys, they have clawlike nails that help them cling to tree trunks.

In all, there are about 250 species of monkeys, the majority of which live in tropical forests. Most eat either fruit or leaves, but a few species, such as capuchins, feed on all sorts of food, from shellfish to insects and small frogs.

Aping About

Many people think apes are large monkeys, but they are different in lots of ways. Apes don't have tails, and while monkeys usually have long back legs and shorter arms, most apes have arms longer than their legs. Monkeys are good at scampering along branches and jumping from tree to tree, but apes climb more slowly, using their strong arms to grip the tree trunk. Gibbons are an exception, though—they use their long arms to swing below the branches.

Orangutans are red-haired apes that live on only two islands in Southeast Asia. These gentle giants spend their whole lives in the

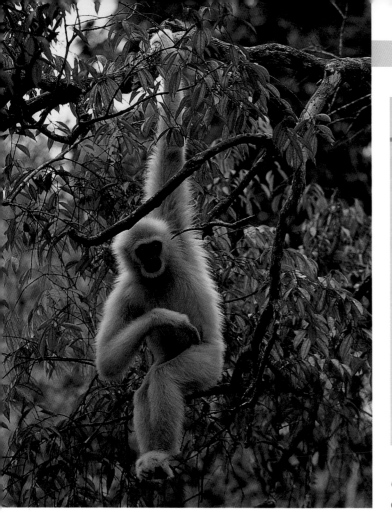

Gibbons can move at tremendous speed through the canopy by swinging underhand from branch to branch.

trees—they find it hard to walk on the ground because their feet are turned inward for holding branches. At night, orangutans weave beds out of twigs and branches high in the trees. The other apes— chimpanzees and gorillas—live in large groups in the forests of Central Africa. They spend most of their time on the ground, though

Gorillas are the largest of the primates. They are highly endangered due to poaching and loss of forest.

they also often sleep in beds woven out of tree branches. Only one species of ape lives outside tropical forests: humans.

Fellow Travelers

Primates are by no means the only mammals in tropical forests. Like most other types of forest, tropical forests are also home to all sorts of rodents—animals like mice, rats, and squirrels. Most rodents are small, but in South American forests a few species have evolved into giants. The agouti is a shy, secretive rodent that searches the forest floor for fallen fruit. At 0.6 meters (2 feet) long, it

The clouded leopard is a wild cat from Southeast Asia. In 2007, zoologists classified the clouded leopards of Borneo and Sumatra as a separate species.

highlands around the Amazon basin. Unlike their fiercer cousins, tropical bears do not hunt large animals. Instead, they eat a mixed diet of fruit, roots, leaves, and insects.

The top **predators** of the forest are the cats. The most famous forest cat is the tiger, which once lived throughout Asia. This wonderful animal is now very rare and survives only in small, protected pockets of forest. Tigers are so big and powerful that they will prey on anything they can catch, even small elephants and rhinoceroses. A few develop a taste for human flesh and become maneaters.

Other forest-dwelling cats include leopards and ocelots, both of which have spots that help them hide from enemies and prey in the dappled shade. Like most big cats, leopards

is so big that many people mistake it for a small deer. Its relative the capybara is even bigger—it grows to more than 1.2 meters (4 feet) long and can weigh as much as a person, making it the biggest rodent in the world. Capybaras are good swimmers and usually live close to rivers, lakes, or marshes. Local people call them water pigs, but they are more closely related to rats than pigs.

Other forest mammals include bears and hoofed animals, such as deer and cattle. Tropical bears are much smaller than the giant hunters of colder areas. Sun bears live in Southeast Asian forests; honey bears, named for their favorite food, live in India and Sri Lanka; while spectacled bears live in cool forests in the

Jaguars are often heard but seldom seen in the tropical forests of Latin America. They are solitary animals and often become aggressive when they meet each other.

39

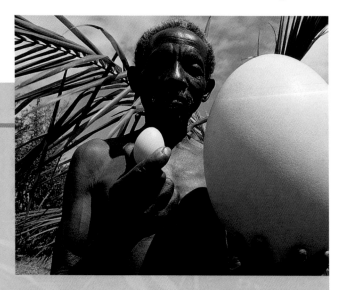

Few parrots are as colorful as the rainbow lorikeet of eastern and northern Australia. Lorikeets are small parrots with brush-tipped tongues for sipping nectar.

Hello, Polly

Tropical forests can seem like unbroken stretches of green, but there are occasional splashes of color. Among the most colorful inhabitants are parrots—large, noisy birds that generally have curved beaks for cracking nuts and cutting fruits. Some parrots have magnificent long tails. The largest parrot of all is the hyacinth macaw of Brazil, which grows to 1 meter (39 inches) from head to tail.

Parrots are often known by different names. Macaws, cockatoos, lorikeets, and parakeets are all different types of parrots, for example. Unlike most birds, parrots have two forward-pointing toes and two backward-pointing ones. This allows a parrot to lift food to its mouth with one foot while clinging to a branch with the other.

Birds are especially common in the forests of New Guinea and Australia, where there are fewer mammals with which to compete.

have declined in numbers because of habitat loss and hunting by humans. However, they are still relatively common in Africa and Asia. When they make a kill, leopards haul the victim's mutilated body into a tree to hide it from other animals. There are no leopards in South America, but the stockier jaguar fills a similar niche.

 Gone Forever

The island of Madagascar used to have some of the most amazing animals in the world—before people arrived and started cutting down the forests. One was the elephant bird, a gigantic, flightless bird nearly twice as tall as a person and weighing 450 kilograms (1,000 pounds). Even the egg of an elephant bird was enormous, as 1,000-year-old specimens (right) found buried in sand have proved. Scientists think the elephant bird fed on the bodies of dead animals, and it may have survived on Madagascar until as recently as 1,100 years ago. Some Arabic and Persian myths describe a terrifying, giant bird called the roc. Perhaps these stories were based on reports from merchants who once sailed from Arabia to the waters around Madagascar.

The emerald tree boa hangs from branches in the Amazon, impersonating vines. It kills small animals by wrapping around them and squeezing until they suffocate; then it swallows them whole.

These snakes are just two of thousands of **reptile** species, including geckos, chameleons, monitor lizards, rattlesnakes, vipers, tree pythons, and boa constrictors, that live in tropical forests. Snakes that live in trees tend to have long, slender bodies that can drape across flimsy branches without falling through. Geckos have sticky feet that let them run up vertical trunks or even along the bottom of branches. And chameleons have strange, pincerlike feet that allows them to grip branches as they creep along.

New Guinea is home to the birds of paradise. Male birds of paradise are brightly colored and adorned with wild headdresses and long tails—all to impress the females.

A strange bird lives in the flooded forests of Ecuador and Peru. It looks a little like a turkey, but it has a blue face and a punk hairstyle of feathers. What makes this bird unique is that the young chicks have claws on their growing wings, which they use for clinging to trees. This prehistoric feature is probably a leftover from the distant reptilian ancestors that birds evolved from: dinosaurs.

Wriggling Reptiles

The largest snakes in the world live in tropical forests. The green anaconda is the heaviest and lives in swampy parts of South America, including the Amazon. The longest snake is the reticulated python, which can reach nearly 10 meters (32 feet).

Hoatzins are known by local people as stink birds because of their disgusting smell.

Left: The strawberry poison-dart frogs of Central America are tiny, growing to only 2.5 centimeters (1 inch) long. To attract females, males inflate their throats and make a trilling sound. The tadpoles develop in puddles or pools of water in bromeliad plants.

Wet and Wild

Amphibians are animals such as frogs, toads, and salamanders that live partly in water and partly on land. They need to keep their skin moist when they are out of water, so the damp climate of a rain forest is perfect for them. The many pools, puddles, and slow-flowing rivers provide countless sites for the tadpoles to develop.

The Panamanian golden frog is now extinct in the wild. In recent years, a fungal disease has placed hundreds of amphibian species at risk of extinction.

Frogs are so common in rain forests that their strange calls, which range from croaks to bleeps, often fill the air at night. Some tropical frogs have beautiful skin colors and patterns that warn predators that they are poisonous. The poison-dart frogs of the Amazon have the most spectacular colors, but also the most deadly poison. The most dangerous species is called the terrible poison-dart frog of western Colombia—a single lick of its skin can kill you. Forest people use the skin of this frog to poison their arrow tips for hunting.

Other amazing forest frogs include the tree frogs, which have sticky disks on their toes that help them cling to leaves and branches. Some tree

Right: Blue poison frogs live only in southern Suriname. They are ravenous eaters, preying on fruit flies, termites, crickets, and ants. Their striking color has made them popular pets—many are now bred in captivity.

Wallace's flying frogs use their webbed feet and skin flaps between their legs to glide up to 15 meters (50 feet) between trees in the forests of Borneo.

frogs lay their eggs in trees, gluing them to the undersides of leaves overhanging water. When the tadpoles have developed, they drop into the water below. Flying frogs are tree frogs with webbed feet and skin flaps that act like wings, enabling them to glide great distances after leaping from a tree.

Leaf-cutter ants use leaf cuttings to grow an edible fungus inside their nests. The ants remove more plant matter than any other type of animal in the forests of Central and South America.

Insects and Spiders

Large animals might be exciting to spot, but they are insignificant in number compared to the insects and other **invertebrates** that teem over every surface in a tropical forest.

Forest insects range from huge, spike-covered crickets to shiny beetles that appear to be made of metal. There are tiny wasps that live inside plants, butterflies bigger than your hand, and all sorts of insects disguised as twigs, leaves, thorns, or flecks of dirt. The wandering spiders of Brazil are perhaps the world's most dangerous spiders. They wander into houses and attack people with little provocation— and a single bite can kill.

Tropical forests are home to the world's biggest insects. Top prize for the heaviest insect goes to the goliath beetle of Africa's Congo rain forest. It grows to 11 centimeters (4.3 inches) long and can weigh up to 100 grams (3.5 ounces). The longest insect is *Pharnacia serratipes*, a stick insect

Below: Goliath beetles of Africa are the world's heaviest insects. When they are in flight they sound like miniature helicopters.

Each leg ends in a pair of claws, or tarsi, used for gripping tree trunks or other surfaces.

Male goliaths have horns for fighting.

ACTUAL SIZE

— *wing case*

When the wings are not in use, they fold away under protective wing cases.

Wallace's Line

N

PHILIPPINES

BRUNEI
MALAYSIA

Borneo

Sulawesi

Wallace's Line

*Pacific
Ocean*

New
Guinea

PAPUA NEW
GUINEA

*Indian
Ocean*

Sumatra

INDONESIA

Java

Bali

Lombok

EAST TIMOR

AUSTRALIA

0   500 miles
0   500   kilometers

If you walked in the footsteps of the explorers and naturalists of the 19th century, through the forests of Malaysia and across to the islands of Indonesia, you might notice changes in the animals around you. You would leave behind the familiar animals such as deer, monkeys, and cats as you left the shores of Bali or Borneo. In Sulawesi and Lombok you would see a mixture of animals from Asia and Australia, but eventually, if you reached New Guinea and Australia, you would see mainly the marsupial mammals that live there, such as tree kangaroos, possums, and

pademelons, a type of wallaby. (North America has its own marsupial—the Virginia opossum.) The famous naturalist Alfred Russel Wallace (1823–1913) drew an imaginary line that divided these characteristic animals of Asia and Australia.

	Pademelon		
Clouded leopard		*Tree kangaroo*	
Sambar		*Bird of paradise*	
Rhesus macaque		*Striped possum*	

from Malaysia that reaches 55.5 centimeters (22 inches) in length—as long as a man's arm.

The leaf litter on the forest floor is alive with tiny animals. Industrious termites and ants play a largely unseen role breaking down dead wood and plants, while scorpions and centipedes patrol in search of food. Without these tiny invertebrates keeping nutrients cycling through the forest, the plants and large animals would not survive for long.

The spiny katydid of the Amazon rain forest is a prickly relative of crickets. Its spiny legs can discourage predators as large as bats and monkeys.

SOUTHEAST ASIA

Southeast Asia has a mixture of rain forest and monsoon forest. People have cleared much of the land to grow crops such as rice, but lush forests survive on many islands and mountains.

Despite a fast rate of logging, Malaysia retains some patches of pristine forest, including those on the slopes of Mount Kinabalu in northern Borneo.

1. Himalayas
The highest mountain range in the world stops the moist monsoon air from reaching farther into Asia and marks the northern edge of the tropical forest.

2. Sri Lanka
Much of the tropical forest that once covered this island has been cleared to make room for tea plantations.

3. Manas Sanctuary
The guards of this tiger sanctuary must constantly battle poachers.

4. Ujung Kulon National Park and Krakatau
This park protects Java's last large patch of forest, where the rare Javan rhino lives—fewer than 100 live wild. It also contains small islands, including the still-smoking cone of Anak Krakatau—son of Krakatau—a volcano that exploded in 1912.

5. Singapore
A city-state and important trade center on an island off the Malaysian peninsula. Its inhabitants come from India, Malaysia, China, and Europe.

Sinharaja Forest Reserve

Fact File

▲ Southeast Asia lies at the meeting point of three of the plates that make up Earth's crust. The movements of these plates have created many mountains, volcanoes, and islands.

▲ Deforestation is occurring at an alarming rate in many of the countries and islands of Southeast Asia, especially Cambodia, Vietnam, Laos, Sumatra, and Borneo. The main causes of deforestation are logging for valuable hardwoods and clearance for farming, palm-oil plantations, or mining.

6. Angkor Wat
A world-famous complex of Hindu and Buddhist temples that rises from the jungle.

7. Cat Ba Island
This small and beautiful national park has diverse habitats, including evergreen rain forests, freshwater swamps, and mangroves.

8. Gunung Mulu
Inside this mountain is a stunning set of limestone caves, including Earth's largest cavern. Over a million bats of many species roost here by day, before leaving at sunset to feast in the forest. The rich plant life in the park around the caves includes 3,500 plant species, 109 of which are palm trees.

9. Kinabalu Park
Visitors like to climb through different kinds of forest to the top of Mount Kinabalu. Invasive dandelion plants have recently been outcompeting native flowers, threatening the natural balance of the park.

10. Maluku
These islands were once called the Spice Islands, and spice crops are still grown there.

Old Man of the Forest

Orangutans used to live all over Southeast Asia but now survive only in patches of forests on the islands of Borneo and Sumatra. With few natural enemies, they grow and breed very slowly. In a lifetime of 45 years, a female orangutan has time to raise only four young, but each baby is cared for intensively. An orangutan mother carries her baby all the time during its first year, and only weans it onto solid food when it is 3 years old. She will not have another youngster for about 8 years. Orangutans, particularly those in Sumatra, are endangered. The threat of their extinction in the wild comes mostly from habitat loss—forest is cleared for palm oil plantations and mining operations—and their capture for the illegal pet trade (right).

PEOPLE AND TROPICAL FORESTS

From the hunter-gatherers of the past to the scientists of today, people have been making use of tropical forests for thousands of years.

The human race evolved in the tropics, so probably there have been people living in tropical forests for as long as our species has existed. The earliest archaeological evidence of settlements in a tropical forest comes from a cave in Sarawak, Malaysia, and dates back 40,000 years. The oldest evidence of people in South American forests is only 5,000 years old, but that's not surprising. The human race did not reach the Americas until about 35,000 years ago, so there are fewer archaeological remains there.

There are still many native peoples living in tropical forests in different parts of the world. Although these groups have many differences, they also share many similarities in the ways in which they live and hunt in the forests.

The Piaroa people of Venezuela still sometimes use blowpipes to hunt monkeys. The darts are tipped with paralyzing poison from the skin of frogs.

The Amazon

We can never know for sure how people lived many thousands of years ago, but it's possible their way of life was similar to that of some modern forest peoples. Most of the native peoples of the Amazon rain forest, for instance, lived until recent times in small communities of hunter-gatherers. Hunter-gatherers are people who collect and hunt their food from the wilderness, instead of growing crops.

A few people still live this way in remote parts of the Amazon, far from towns or roads. They hunt such animals as monkeys, deer, and birds. Today they often use guns for hunting, but in the past they used blowpipes, bows and arrows, nets, or spears to catch prey.

Coconut Palms

The coconut palm is one of the most important crops in the tropics. Their seeds—coconuts—contain a milky drink and a rich, edible flesh, from which a valuable oil is extracted. The thick husks of coconuts yield coir —a very strong fiber used to make ropes, mats, and brooms. The leaves of coconut palms are used for thatching and baskets, the leaf buds are eaten as a salad vegetable, and the trunks are used to construct houses. The sugary sap from coconut flowers can even be made into an alcoholic drink called toddy.

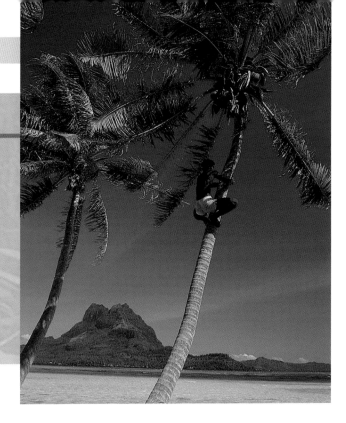

The Congo

Central Africa's Congo rain forest is home to three major groupings of people who live as hunter-gatherers: the Mbuti, Twa, and Mbenga. These people have been called pygmies because they are very short. On average, they are only about 1.2 to 1.4 meters (4 feet to 4 feet 8 inches) tall.

The Mbuti, Twa, and Mbenga hunt elephants and antelopes with small bows that fire poison arrows, and they also gather honey from bees' nests—a dangerous task, given the ferocious temperament of African honey bees. Like the people of the Amazon, the people of the Congo's forest live in small communities and build temporary dwellings in the forest. There is no single leader in a community; instead members have general discussions to try and solve problems. Marriages are arranged between communities, forging family links that tie communities together. People can leave one community to join another whenever they like.

In common with other hunter-gatherer peoples, the Mbuti, Twa, and Mbenga use the forest in a sustainable way. They live off its resources without having to fell the trees, so they do little damage to their environment.

The hunter-gatherer way of life is dying out in the Congo. The forest has been shrinking steadily for centuries because farmers from outside have been cutting down trees to grow crops. Increasingly, the Mbuti, Twa, and Mbenga trade meat with their farming neighbors in exchange for knives, tools, and crops like bananas, corn, and rice.

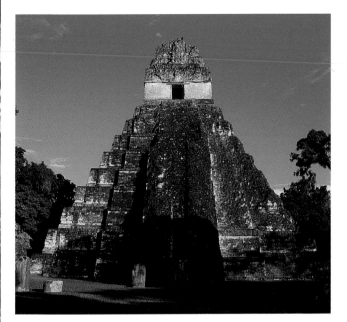

Until about 900 C.E., people of the Mayan civilization built cities in the lowlands of Guatemala. Their temples now stand abandoned, many overgrown by forest.

Beyond Africa

There are forest-living people in Sri Lanka and the Andaman Islands in the Indian Ocean who might be related to the forest people of the Congo. They look more African than Asian and are less than 1.5 meters (5 feet) tall. The Veddahs of Sri Lanka were probably the island's original inhabitants and have lived there for many thousands of years. More recent immigrants from India have since cut down much of Sri Lanka's forests, and the Veddahs are now a tiny group. Scientists believe that the Veddahs and other peoples living in isolated spots throughout the Indian Ocean are descendants of Africans who

Hunting animals is still an important feature of life on Fergusson Island, Papua New Guinea. This wild pig was caught in a trap.

spread to Asia and Australia. Australia and New Guinea's aboriginal people are thought to belong to the same group.

Farming the Tropics

Before the age of agriculture, most of the world's people lived as hunter-gatherers. At some point, however, people learned how to grow crops and raise their own animals. Since then, farming gradually spread around the world, and the hunter-gatherer way of life began to die out. Today, the last few hunter-gatherers live in tough environments where farming is difficult, such as deserts, arid (dry) savannas, or the heart of dense rain forests.

In recent history, most cultures that have thrived in the tropics have lived by farming. To grow their food, farmers often had to clear the land of forest. In Southeast Asia, for instance, rice fields have taken the place of swampy rain forests in many areas. Most of India was once covered with monsoon forest, but today the bare landscape looks like an almost treeless grassland.

Colonial Era

In the 15th century, European sailors began to explore the world. The driving force behind the expeditions was trade. European merchants knew that if they could travel to China and Southeast Asia by sea, they could buy products such as silk and spices more cheaply than by overland routes, which were controlled by Persian and Arab traders.

To a European merchant, a tropical forest was nothing more than a place where spices grew. Spices such as nutmeg, pepper, cinnamon, and cloves were important for cooking in those days because they masked the flavor of poorly preserved meat. But the Spice Islands (present-day Indonesia) were very far away. To get there, sailors had to make a perilous voyage all the way around

The people of Papua New Guinea have used birds of paradise to make ceremonial headdresses for many generations, yet few of the birds are endangered. The main threat facing the island's wildlife is deforestation.

Africa, so they started looking for shortcuts. One such sailor was Christopher Columbus, who thought he could reach the Spice Islands by sailing west. He was wrong, but because of his mistake, Europeans came into contact with the Americas.

Dutch Control

By the 17th century, the Dutch controlled the production of spices in Southeast Asia. They tried to restrict each spice to a single island—they grew nutmeg on one island, pepper on another, and so on. They destroyed the spice trees on all other islands in the area to ensure they would get the highest price for their crop. However, their plan to monopolize the spice trade was foiled by

Jarawa

The Jarawa people live as hunter-gatherers in the rain forests of the Andaman Islands. They have lived in these forests for thousands of years, hunting wild pigs and monitor lizards, catching fish with bows and arrows, and gathering seeds and berries. Their origins are unknown, but scientists think they may have come from Africa rather than Asia.

Today there are fewer than 350 Jarawa left on only two islands. Like other Andaman peoples, they are at risk of being relocated from their homeland by the Indian authorities, who want to "civilize" (or just better control) them. Other peoples that have been moved have been almost wiped out by mainland diseases, such as measles. If the Jarawa are evicted from the forest, they are likely to share this fate.

Attack of the Amazons

The first European to cross the Amazon rain forest was a Spanish explorer named Francisco de Orellana. In 1540, Orellana and a group of conquistadors marched across the Andes mountains east of Quito and reached a roaring waterfall leading to a wide river. They decided to build a sailing boat (which took weeks to construct) and send a group of men downriver to pick up supplies, with Orellana in charge. But Orellana never came back. By the time he found supplies, he had gone too far to turn around, and he faced attacks from hostile Amerindians. In one incident, his group was attacked by what appeared to be female warriors. The Spaniards called the mighty river down which they were sailing the Amazon, after the female warriors of Greek mythology, and the name stuck. It took them about a year to reach the Atlantic—a voyage of some 4,750 kilometers (3,000 miles). After a stop in Trinidad, Orellana finally returned home to Spain.

Tea-pickers collect their harvest on a plantation in Sri Lanka. Only the tips—the youngest leaves—are picked. Tea grows best in places with a humid, rainy climate.

pigeons, which ate the fruits of spice trees and deposited seeds in their droppings on neighboring islands.

By the start of the 20th century, most of the world's tropical forests were under European control, and colonists around the globe began to clear forests for plantations. Spices had already been introduced to Africa; cloves from Indonesia, for example, were being grown on the island of Zanzibar off the coast of Tanzania. Bananas, originally from Asia, were being grown in South America.

Far away, in northern Europe, the demand for forest products increased. Rubber, made from the resin of Amazon rubber trees, became a valuable commodity. As a result, rubber trees were soon growing in Southeast Asia and on Pacific islands. The wealthy Europeans had also started drinking tea and coffee in large quantities, so tea and coffee plantations began to spread, as did plantations to grow sugarcane and cocoa.

Power to the People

Some of the world's largest cities are in the tropics, such as Bangkok in Thailand and São Paulo in Brazil. People have harnessed the heavy tropical rain to provide power for such cities. Hydroelectric power plants use water falling from a dam to generate electricity.

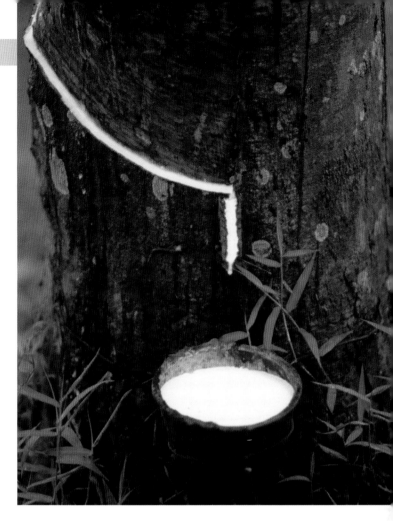

Natural rubber comes from the bark of a tropical tree native to Brazil. A sharp knife is used to cut the bark, then the rubber is collected in cups.

When people build a dam, the water trapped behind it forms a lake. Because many tropical rivers flow through flat land, dams built across them can flood vast areas of forest. Brazil's growing need for hydropower could lead to major new dams being built in the flat Amazon Basin. Such dams can be ecological disasters, however. The water drowns forests, killing plants and animals, and the dams stop fish and turtles from moving to their breeding grounds. The dead plants rot slowly in the water, releasing poisonous chemicals.

Chemical Factories

The plants in tropical forests produce all sorts of poisonous chemicals that protect them from being eaten. Some of these chemicals could turn out to be useful drugs.

 Saving the Planet

In the past, people didn't think twice about cutting down a tropical forest to sell the timber or to farm the land to make money. Today, however, many people want to conserve tropical forests to protect the amazingly diverse wildlife. A good way to do this is to find a way of making the forest pay for itself.

There are several forest products that people can harvest without having to cut down the trees. Many are controlled by governments to make sure the forest wildlife is not damaged by over-zealous harvesting. For example, large leaves are collected from some tropical forests for use as packaging for gifts in the industrialized countries. Similarly, the edible nests of cave-dwelling birds are harvested in Borneo to make bird's nest soup in expensive Asian restaurants.

Many tropical plant chemicals are already used as drugs. The drug quinine, for instance, has long been used to treat malaria, one of the world's biggest killer diseases. Quinine comes from the bark of the cinchona tree of South America, where people have been using it for centuries. When surgeons operate, they sometimes give patients a drug called curare to make their muscles relax. Curare comes from the roots of a South American vine. A more recent discovery was a plant called rosy periwinkle, which grows in the dry forests of Madagascar. It contains a drug that can help treat leukemia (cancer of the blood).

Scientists sometimes use local medicine men or witch doctors to help them find forest plants containing drugs. The witch doctors use many herbs in their healing ceremonies, and some of these could hold cures for AIDS or cancers. Sometimes, however, plants of interest are overcollected and native people exploited by western businesses in the process.

NEW GUINEA

New Guinea is a rugged wilderness of mountains and rain forests. The western half is Irian Jaya, a province of Indonesia. The east is Papua New Guinea, an independent country.

Much of New Guinea is protected by the mountainous landscape, which has, so far, made the forest inaccessible to loggers. Waterfalls tumble off the steep slopes, such as this one near Tari.

Birds of Paradise

In the 16th century, Spanish sailors completed the first ever round-the-world trip. Among the exotic treasures they brought home were stuffed birds with flamboyant feathers that became known as birds of paradise. It was many years before scientists studied these birds in the wild, but they soon discovered that only the males sport bright colors, long tails, and headdresses. They use their showy plumage to attract females in the gloom of the forest.

Fact File

▲ More than two-thirds of New Guinea is cloaked in dense rain forest, sustained by the island's very high rainfall.

▲ The wildlife of New Guinea is more like that of Australia than Southeast Asia. Most of the mammals are marsupials—mammals that carry their young in pouches.

▲ New Guinea is home to the cassowary, a large and dangerous flightless bird that can seriously injure or even kill a person with its powerful kick.

▲ If the present rate of deforestation in New Guinea continues, all its rain forest will be logged by 2030.

1. Puncak Jaya
The tallest mountain in New Guinea, with a peak of 5,040 meters (16,535 feet). Unusually for tropical mountains, Puncak Jaya and its neighbors are snowcapped.

2. Lorentz National Park
The largest protected area in Southeast Asia. It includes a range of tropical habitats, from snowcapped mountains to coastal wetlands.

3. Mangrove Swamps
Dense mangrove swamps fringe the southern coast. About one-third of the mangrove swamps have been cut down in the last 20 years.

4. Southern Lowlands
Freshwater swamp forests flourish in the lowlands. In scattered places are dense stands of klinki pines. These close relatives of monkey puzzles are the world's tallest tropical trees.

5. Torres Strait
New Guinea was joined to Australia until as recently as 8,000 years ago, when rising seas flooded the Torres Strait.

6. Northern Lowlands
The rain forests of northern New Guinea are home to Scott's tree kangaroo, New Guinea's largest native mammal and endangered by habitat loss.

It has a strong smell that can linger for a week on a person who touches the animal.

7. Fly River
One of New Guinea's longest rivers, the Fly carries huge amounts of sediment washed off the steep mountains by heavy rain. The sediment provides nourishment for the coastal mangrove swamps.

8. Cape York Pensinula
Rain forest hugs the east coast of Cape York Peninsula, the most northerly part of Australia. The forest is home to numerous orchids and some of the same animal species as New Guinea, including two birds of paradise.

9. Great Barrier Reef
The northern tip of this vast system of coral reefs reaches up toward the Gulf of Papua. Global warming is threatening the survival of all coral reefs.

10. Mount Wilhelm
The tallest mountain in Papua New Guinea, at 4,509 meters (14,793 feet) high.

11. New Britain and New Ireland
Rain-drenched, forested islands forming part of Papua New Guinea. West New Britain gets 6 meters (20 feet) of rain each year. Deforestation for the logging of valuable hardwoods threatens these ancient forests.

THE FUTURE

The world's tropical forests are disappearing rapidly, and many of their species are becoming extinct. Fortunately, there are lots of ways we can help protect the forests.

In 1850, the world's population was about a billion; today it stands at about 6.8 billion. According to the United Nations, the world's population could reach 9 billion by 2040 if people keep having babies at the same rate. What does all this mean for the tropical forests of the world?

Many areas of tropical forest are in developing countries, where the population, though relatively low, is increasing fastest. Life can be difficult for people in developing countries. In some cases, people have little choice but to cut down the forests and use the land to raise cattle or grow crops. Every year, an area of tropical forest the size of West Virginia is cut down by settlers who move to the forest to farm. If **deforestation** continues at this rate, the world's tropical forests could disappear in less than 100 years.

Starting Point

Settlers were not the first people to start damaging the forest—loggers in search of huge hardwood trees came first. The best hardwoods are used to make high-quality furniture, which is often exported to industrialized countries, but most timber from tropical forests is used

? Saving the Planet

One way to make a rain forest pay for its own protection is to invite paying tourists to take a vacation there. Tourists can now stay in floating hotels on the Amazon River or walk through the canopy of cloud forests in Costa Rica (right). People who go on such trips are called ecotourists, and the money they spend helps preserve the rain forest. Ecotourists have to follow strict rules to keep the environment healthy—after all, that's what they've come to see.

Commercial logging—both legal and illegal—is one of the biggest threats facing the Amazon rain forest.

for beams in houses across the world. Logging is a big business that is worth billions a year worldwide. A 1-meter (39-inches) cube of tropical hardwood can fetch up to $1,000.

Early loggers cleared large trees from the edges of forests. Later, logging companies began cutting roads into the forests to get at the huge trees in the interior. These roads let settlers move deeper into the forest to start farms, speeding up the deforestation.

Slash and Burn

For thousands of years, people living in the forest have cleared small areas to use as vegetable gardens. The traditional way of doing this is to cut the trees down and burn them, a technique called slash and burn. The ash from the burned trees is rich in minerals and enriches the soil for a few years. But after three or four years, the minerals run out and the soil becomes poor. This happens very quickly in the tropics because the soil is thin and plants use up nutrients rapidly. So the farmer clears another patch of trees and lets the old land turn back into forest.

In recent times, settlers from outside the forest have used the same method on a much bigger scale. Because there are more mouths to feed, the settlers clear bigger areas and farm the land for as long as possible. Abandoned farms get reused after just a few years, instead of being left to revert to forest. This way of farming weakens the land so much that full tropical forest may not recover for centuries. Instead, patchy woodlands with small trees and dusty grasslands take its place.

Even where dense forest does grow back, it is secondary forest, with fewer species than the original primary forest.

Centuries of Damage

When done carefully, logging does not cause a huge amount of damage to tropical forests and could be a good way of making money to protect them. Within a hundred years, the gap left by a felled tree fills up again, and only experts can tell that logging took place. However, clearing land for ranches or plantations can ruin it. Experts estimate that it would take the best part of 1,000 years for tropical forests to grow back in such places.

Clearing forests for cattle ranches (left) and floods created by dams (below) both contribute to deforestation in the Amazon. According to the government of Brazil, 14 percent of Brazilian Amazon forest has been lost since 1970, and the rate of deforestation is speeding up.

Pacific Ocean

Atlantic Ocean

N

0 ————— 1,000 miles
0 ——1,000—— kilometers

Amazon basin

SOUTH AMERICA

Under Threat

Impenetrable jungle and vast swamps once made most of the Amazon rain forest out of bounds to all but the most intrepid explorers or the resident population of native South Americans. Today, things are very different. Speedboats and new highways have opened up the region to developers, loggers, miners, and farmers, and the landscape is changing fast. This map shows areas that still contain primary (undisturbed) rain forest (dark green) not currently threatened by destruction. The red zone is primary forest at high risk of deforestation, and pale green is farmland and secondary forest—the impoverished forest that grows back after deforestation.

- *Primary forest not at immediate risk.*
- *Primary forest threatened by deforestation.*
- *Deforested land covered by farmland and secondary forest*

Even 1,000 years might not be long enough for some stretches of deforested land. When a tropical forest is cut down, there is nothing to protect the thin soil from the sun, wind, and pouring rain. The tropical sunshine turns the soil to dust, and heavy rain washes it away, leaving deep gashes in the countryside. This process, called **soil erosion**, can make the land look more like a desert than a jungle.

Changing Climate

Just as the climate affects what grows in tropical forests, so the forest can affect the climate. Thick forests packed with trees release huge amounts of water that the plants have sucked up from the ground and given out through their leaves. The water vapor rising from the forest produces clouds, adding to the region's rainfall.

With the forest and the water vapor gone, there is less rain—and less cloud to shield the ground from the scorching Sun. The once-rich soil turns into dust and blows away or bakes

Sustainable Forests

Chopping down trees is not the only way to make money from a tropical forest. There are several ways the land can be used to grow food and other products without the forest being damaged beyond repair. The techniques currently being tested around the world are a mixture of new ideas and methods that have been used by local people for thousands of years.

Crops can be grown in combination with trees, which shade plants from the strong sunshine; coffee tastes even better when grown in the shade. Trees also provide support for vine crops, such as pepper and vanilla plants. Another way of conserving the forest is to plant a row of trees and shrubs around a field of crops. This green fence provides firewood, food for cattle, protects the crops from wind and strong sunshine, and a home for the smaller animals of the tropical forests.

Of course, it is also important to set aside areas where all farming, logging, and other destructive practices are banned. These reserves are refuges for rare animals and plants, and they soak up rainwater, helping protect neighboring areas from erosion.

into a crust. Scientists have discovered that smoke from the fires started by slash-and-burn farmers can speed up this process by stopping rain clouds from forming.

Another climatic change caused in part by deforestation is more far-reaching. When trees are cut down or burned, they release carbon dioxide—one of the gases that causes global warming. High in the **atmosphere**, carbon dioxide traps heat radiating from the ground, making the planet warm up. The process is called the greenhouse effect because it is similar to the way glass windows trap heat in a greenhouse. People have already released masses of carbon dioxide into the atmosphere by burning wood, coal, gas, and oil; deforestation makes the problem worse.

Tapirs are famous for their ability to walk on riverbeds to escape from jaguars. These shy, short-sighted animals are dying out because of hunting and deforestation.

Endangered Species

Nobody knows how many species live in tropical forests, so nobody knows how many are being wiped out. Some scientists estimate that several hundred unique rain-forest species disappear every day. Hunting, pollution, deforestation, and the fragmentation of forest caused by the building of roads all put pressure on the survival of wild animals and plants. Once a species is extinct, it is lost forever, making our planet a less interesting place. Species rely on each other to survive and if we lose one, we will lose the species that depend on it, and so on. At its worst, one day there may be little more than rats, cockroaches, weeds, and humans left.

The destruction of tropical forests is threatening so many of Earth's animals, including tigers, proboscis monkeys, aye-ayes, and tapirs. These are just the species we know about—many more plants and insects are being destroyed before scientists get the chance to name them, before doctors can test them for medicines, or before anyone can even look at them.

The Eden Project is a bold attempt to re-create an area of rain forest under a vast, dome-shaped greenhouse in England. Although such projects conserve few species, they help raise public awareness about deforestation.

 The Golden Lion Tamarin

The stories of Brazil's tropical forests are not all bad. One that has a relatively happy ending is the story of the golden lion tamarin. This hamster-sized monkey is named for its luxurious golden fur and handsome mane. By the 1980s, its forest home on the coast of Brazil had almost disappeared, and the tamarin was on the verge of extinction. Its plight caught the attention of conservationists around the world, and a program of breeding in zoos was started.

Tamarins raised in zoos across the world were soon being released into protected forests in Brazil. The first few monkeys had been raised in cages with branches fixed to the walls—they had never moved through a wild tree that swayed under their own weight. Tragically, most fell from the treetops to their deaths. From then on, conservationists made sure captive tamarins lived in trees, which helped them adjust to the wild after being released. Now, thanks to many years of hard work, golden lion tamarins have a chance to escape the threat of extinction.

GLOSSARY

amphibian: An animal, such as a frog, toad, or salamander, that lives partly in water and partly on land.

atmosphere: The layer of air around Earth.

biome: A major division of the living world, distinguished by its climate and wildlife. Tundra, desert, and temperate grassland are examples of biomes.

canopy: The rooflike layer of treetops in a dense forest.

carbon dioxide: A gas released when fuel burns. Carbon dioxide is one of the main gases thought to cause global warming.

chlorophyll: A green chemical in the leaves and stems of plants that captures the energy in sunlight and helps convert it to food.

climate: The pattern of weather that happens in one place during an average year.

cloud forest: A type of tropical forest that grows on mountains and is often foggy or misty.

cold-blooded: Having a body temperature that depends on the surroundings.

deciduous: Describes a plant that sheds its leaves periodically.

deforestation: The clearing of forest, usually carried out by cutting down or burning trees.

equator: An imaginary line around Earth, midway between the North and South poles.

epiphyte: A plant that grows on another plant and gets its water from the air or from rain.

erosion: The gradual wearing away of land by the action of wind, rain, rivers, ice, or the sea.

evaporate: To turn into gas. When water evaporates, it becomes an invisible part of the air.

evolve: To change gradually over many generations. All the world's species have formed through evolution.

fertile: Capable of sustaining plant growth. Farmers often try to make soil more fertile when growing crops.

hunter-gatherer: A person who obtains food by hunting, fishing, and foraging rather than farming.

infertile: Soil that is unable to support plentiful plant life is termed infertile.

invertebrate: An animal that has no backbone, such as a worm, insect, or spider.

ivory: A hard white material that forms the tusks of elephants.

mammal: A warm-blooded animal that feeds its young on milk. Mice, bats, and whales are all mammals.

mangrove: A tree that grows in swamps on tropical coasts. Many mangroves have prop roots that support them.

marsupial: A type of mammal in which the young develop in a pouch on the mother's body.

microclimate: The pattern of weather within a small area, such as a valley, treetop, or burrow.

monsoon: A very rainy season in South Asia; or the wind that causes the rainy season.

nectar: A sugary liquid produced by a plant to attract the animals that pollinate its flowers.

niche: The particular way of life and habitat of a species.

nocturnal: Active at night.

nutrient: Any chemical that nourishes plants or animals, helping them grow. Plants absorb nutrients from the soil, while animals get nutrients from food.

oxygen: A gas in the air. Animals and plants need to take in oxygen so their cells can release energy from food.

parasite: An organism that lives inside or on another organism and harms it.

photosynthesis: The chemical process that plants use to make food from simple chemicals and the Sun's energy.

pollen: A dustlike powder made by the male parts of flowers that makes seeds with female parts.

pollination: The transfer of pollen from the male part of a flower to the female part of the same flower or another flower.

predator: An animal that catches and eats other animals.

primate: A type of mammal that usually has grasping hands and forward-facing eyes. Most primates live in the trees of tropical forests.

rain forest: A lush forest that receives frequent heavy rainfall. Tropical rain forests grow in the tropics; temperate rain forests grow in cooler places.

reptile: A cold-blooded animal such as a snake, lizard, crocodile, or turtle that usually has scaly skin and moves either on its belly or on short legs.

reserve: A protected area for wildlife.

savanna: Tropical grassland dotted with trees.

sediment: Particles of sand or mud carried by a river.

seed: A small, protective body containing a baby plant.

soil erosion: Removal of soil from land by the action of wind and rain. Soil erosion often happens after deforestation.

species: A particular type of organism. Cheetahs are a species, for instance, but birds are not, because there are lots of different bird species.

swamp: A shallow wetland full of trees that can grow in water.

temperate: Having a moderate climate. Earth's temperate zones are situated between the warm tropical regions and the cold polar regions.

tropic of Cancer: An imaginary line around Earth 2,600 kilometers (1,600 miles) north of the equator. There, the Sun is directly overhead at noon on June 21.

tropic of Capricorn: An imaginary line around Earth 2,600 kilometers (1,600 miles) south of the equator.

tropical: Between the tropics of Cancer and Capricorn. Tropical countries are warm all year.

tropical forest: Forest in Earth's tropical zone, such as tropical rain forest or seasonal tropical forest.

tropical grassland: A tropical biome that mainly contains grassland, such as savanna.

venom: A poison injected by an animal using fangs or a sting.

warm-blooded: Having a constantly warm body temperature. Mammals and birds are warm-blooded.

Further Research

Books

Allaby, M. and R. Garrat. *Tropical Forests (Biomes of the Earth)*. New York: Chelsea Clubhouse, 2006.
Dunbar, Robin, and L. Barrett. *Cousins—Our Primate Relatives*. New York: DK Publishing, 2001.
Johansson, Philip. *The Tropical Rain Forest: A Web of Life*. Berkeley Heights. N. J.: Enslow, 2004.
Marcus, Bernard A. *Tropical Forests*. Sudbury, Mass.: Jones & Bartlett, 2008.
Moore, P. and R. Garrat. *Tropical Forests (Ecosystem)*. New York: Facts on File, 2007.
Prance, Ghillean. *Rainforests of the World: Water, Fire, Earth, and Air*. New York: Random House, 1998.

Websites

Wild World—Ecological Regions of the World: www.nationalgeographic.com/wildworld/terrestrial.html
(A huge resource from National Geographic and the Worldwide Fund for Nature. Through a clickable map, you can access pictures and profiles of hundreds of ecoregions, which are like smaller divisions of biomes.)
Rainforestweb: www.rainforestweb.org
(Links to sites about rain-forest conservation.)
Learning About Rainforests: www.srl.caltech.edu/personnel/krubal/rainforest/Edit560s6/www/what.html
(Useful site with introductory information about rain-forest ecosystems.)
Rainforest Facts: www.rain-tree.com/facts.htm
(Collection of interesting facts about rain forests.)

INDEX

Picture Credits